Mel Bay's 100 GOSPEL FAVORITES for Guitar

By Bill Bay

The songs contained in this collection comprise both traditional gospel favorites and new songs. The emphasis throughout this book was on choosing uplifting, victorious songs which convey the positive message of the Christian faith. All songs were arranged for two-part vocal singing with guitar accompaniment. The guitar accompaniment parts are written in notation and in tablature and may be played with a pick or in fingerstyle. It is hoped that this book is a useful worship resource for any guitarist involved in Christian music and worship.

Bill Bay

PSALM 150:4

. . . . . . *praise him with stringed instruments* . . . . . .

Contents

How to Read Tablature

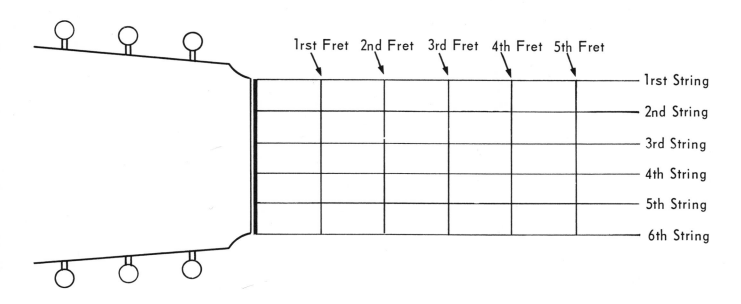

In Tablature the lines Represent Strings. The numbers appearing on the lines indicate Frets. (o = open string) In the following Example a C chord would be played. (1st String Open, 2nd String press Down on the 1st Fret, 3rd String Open, 4th String press down on the 2nd Fret, 5th String press down on the 3rd Fret, and Finally do not play the 6th String.)

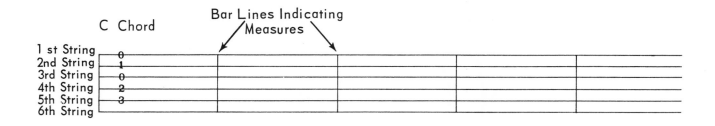

Rhythm in Tablature

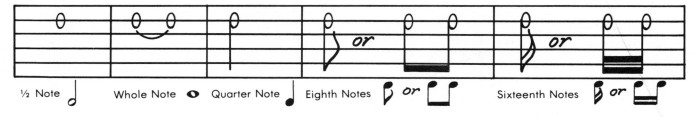

*Master Chord Reference Chart on pages 110 & 111

How Great Is Our God

How great is our God! How great is His name.

How great is our God! _____ For ev - er the same!

He rolled back the wa - ters of the might-y Red Sea,

And He said, "I'll nev-er leave you, Put your trust in Me!

Daily, Daily Sing The Praises

Verses by Sabine Baring-Gould
Chorus by Wm. Bay

Wm. Bay

Lily Of The Valley

Charles W. Fry
1837-1882

From Williams. Hays
1837-1907

1. I've found a friend in Je - sus, He's ev - 'ry - thing to me, He's the
2. He all my griefs has ta - ken, and all my sor - row borne; In temp -
3. He'll nev - er, nev - er leave me, nor yet for - sake me here, While I

fair - est of ten thou - sand to my soul; The Lil - y of the Val - ley, in
ta - tion He's my strong and might - y tower; I have all for Him for - sa - ken, and
live by faith and do His bless - ed will; A wall of fire a - bout me, I've

Him a - lone I see All I need to cleanse and make me ful - ly whole.
all my i - dols torn From my heart, and now He keeps me by His pow'r.
noth - ing now to fear, With His man - na He my hun - gry soul shall fill.

Chorus

In sor - row He's my com - fort, in trou - ble He's my stay; He
Tho' all the world for - sake me, and Sa - tan tempt me sore, Thru
Then sweep - ing up to glo - ry to see His bless - ed face, Where

6

My God, How Great Thou Art

F. W. Faber From
"Spiritual Songs"

Adapt. From
Damon's Psalmes, 1579

tells me ev-'ry care on Him to roll:
He's the Lil-y of the Val-ley the

Je-sus I shall safe-ly reach the goal:

riv-ers of de-light shall ev-er roll:

Bright and Morn-ing Star, He's the fair-est of ten thou-sand to my soul!

1. My God, how great Thou art, Thy maj-es-ty how bright! How
2. I love Thee too, O Lord, Al-might-y as Thou art; For
3. No one can love like Thee, No moth-er half so mild For-
4. My God, how great Thou art, Thou ev-er-last-ing Friend! On

glo-rious is Thy mer-cy seat, In depths of burn-ing light!
Thou hast stooped to ask of me The love of my poor heart.
gives and loves as Thou hast done With me, Thy sin-ful child.
Thee I stay my trust-ing heart, Till faith in vis-ion end. A - men.

The Fire Is Burning

Johnson Oatman, Jr.
1856-1922

George L. Hugg
1848-1907

1. I've been on Mount Pis-gah's loft-y height, And I've sat-is-fied my long-ing heart's de-sire;
2. I will walk with Je-sus, bless His name, And to be like Him I ev-'ry day as-pire;
3. I my all up-on the al-tar lay, As I to my clos-et lov-ing-ly re-tire;

For I caught a glimpse of glo-ry bright, And my soul is burn-ing with the fire!
For His love is like a heav'n-ly flame, And my soul is burn-ing with the fire!
And the flame con-sumes while there I pray, And my soul is burn-ing with the fire!

Chorus

O the fire is burn-ing, yes, 'tis bright-ly burn-ing, O 'tis burn-ing, burn-ing in my soul;

O the fire is burn-ing, yes, 'tis bright-ly burn-ing, O 'tis burn-ing, burn-ing in my soul.

This Is The Day

Composer Unknown

Joyful tempo

This is the day, this is the day that the Lord has made, that the Lord has made.

We will re-joice, we will re-joice and be glad in it and be glad in it.

This is the day that the Lord hath made. We will re-joice and be glad in it.

This is the day, this is the day that the Lord hath made.

He Abides

Herbert Buffum

D. M. Shanks

1. I'm re-joic - ing night and day, As I walk the pil - grim way, For the
2. Once my heart was full of sin, Once I had no peace with - in, Till I
3. He is with me ev - 'ry-where, And He knows my ev - 'ry care, I'm as

hand of God in all my life I see, And the rea-son of my bliss, Yes, the se-cret all is this: That the
heard how Je-sus died up - on the tree; Then I fell down at His feet, And there came a peace so sweet, Now the
hap-py as a bird and just as free; For the Spir-it has con-trol, Je - sus sat - is - fies my soul, Since the

Chorus

Com-fort-er a-bides with me.
Com-fort-er a-bides with me.
Com-fort-er a-bides with me.

He a-bides, He a-bides, Hal-le-lu-jah, He a-bides with

me! I'm re-joic-ing night and day, As I walk the nar-row way, For the Com-fort-er a-bides with me.

10

Jesus Saves

Priscilla J. Owens
1829-1907

William J. Kirkpatrick
1838-1921

Yesterday, Today, Forever

Albert B. Simpson
1843-1919

James H. Burke
19th Century

1. Oh, how sweet the glo-rious mes-sage, Sim-ple faith may claim;
2. Oft on earth He healed the suf-f'rer By His might-y hand;

Yes-ter-day, to-day, for-ev-er, Je-sus is the same.
Still our sick-ness-es and sor-rows Go at His com-mand.

Still He loves to save the sin-ful, Heal the sick and lame;
He who gave His heal-ing vir-tue, To a wom-an's touch;

Cheer the mourn-er, still the tem-pest; Glo-ry to His name.
To the faith that claims His full-ness, Still will give as much

Chorus

Yes-ter-day, to-day, for-ev-er, Je-sus is the same,
All may change, but Jesus nev-er! Glo-ry to His name.
Glo-ry to His name, Glo-ry to His name;
All may change, but Jesus nev-er! Glo-ry to His name!

Glory To His Name

Elisha A. Hoffman,
1839-1929

John H. Stockton
1813-1877

1. Down at the cross where my Sav - ior died, Down where for cleans-ing from
2. I am so won - drous-ly saved from sin, Je - sus so sweet-ly a -
3. Oh, pre - cious foun - tain that saves from sin, I am so glad I have

sin I cried, There to my heart was the blood ap - plied; Glo - ry to His name.
bides with - in; There at the cross where He took me in; Glo - ry to His name.
en - tered in; There Je - sus saves me and keeps me clean; Glo - ry to His name.

Refrain

Glo - ry to His name, Glo - ry to His name.

There to my heart was the blood ap - plied; Glo - ry to His name. A - men.

Heavenly Father, We Appreciate You

Source Unknown

1. Heav-en-ly Fa - ther, we ap-pre-ci-ate You. Hea-ven-ly
2. Son of God, I mag - ni - fy You. Son of
3. Ho - ly Spir - it, what a com - fort You are. Ho - ly

Fa - ther, we ap-pre - ci - ate You. We
God I mag - ni - fy You. You've
Spir - it what a com - fort You are. You

love You, a - dore You, we bow down be - fore You. Heav-en - ly
cleansed me from sin, and sent the Spir - it with in. Son of
lead us You guide us; sent You live right in - side us, Ho - ly

Fa - ther, we ap-pre - ci - ate You.
God, I mag - ni - fy You.
Spir - it what I com - fort You are. A - men.

15

I Believed The True Report

C. P. Jones

1. I've be - lieved the true re - port, Hal - le - lu - jah to the Lamb! I have
2. I'm a king and priest to God, Hal - le - lu - jah to the Lamb! By the
3. I'm with - in the hol - iest pale, Hal - le - lu - jah to the Lamb! I have

passed the out - er court, O glo - ry be to God! I am all on Je - sus' side, On the
cleans - ing of the blood, O glo - ry be to God! By the Spir - it's pow'r and light, I am
passed the in - ner vail O glo - ry be to God! I am sanc - ti - fied to God By the

al - tar sanc - ti - fied, To the world and sin I've died, Hal - le - lu - jah to the Lamb!
liv - ing day and night, In the ho - liest place so bright, Hal - le - lu - jah to the Lamb!
pow - er of the blood, Now the Lord is my a - bode, Hal - le - lu - jah to the Lamb!

Chorus

Hal - le - lu - jah! Hal - le - lu - jah! I have passed the riv - en vail, where the

Jesus Breaks Every Fetter

Composer Unknown

1. Je - sus breaks ev - 'ry fet - ter, Je - sus breaks ev - 'ry fet - ter, Je - sus
2. I will shout Hal - le - lu - jah! I will shout Hal - le - lu - jah! I will
3. I will give God the glo - ry, I will give God the glo - ry, I will

breaks ev - 'ry fet - ter, And He sets me free.
shout Hal - le - lu - jah, For He sets me free.
give God the glo - ry, For He sets me free.

Glory To God, Hallelujah

Fanny J. Crosby
1820-1915
Vs. 3 W. Bay

Wm J. Kirkpatrick
1838-1921

1. We are nev - er, nev - er wea - ry of the grand old song;
2. We are lost a - mid the rap - ture of re - deem - ing love;
3. By God's Spir - it we are ov - er com - ing Sa - tan's pow'r;

Glo - ry to God, Hal - le - lu - jah! We can sing it loud as ev - er, with our
Glo - ry to God, Hal - le - lu - jah! We are ris - ing on its pin - ions to the
Glo - ry to God, Hal - le - lu - jah! In God's word we find His prom - is - es for

faith more strong: Glo - ry to God Hal - le - lu - jah!
hills a - bove, Glo - ry to God Hal - le - lu - jah!
us each hour: Glo - ry to God Hal - le - lu - jah!

Chorus

O, the chil - dren of the Lord have a right to shout and sing, For the

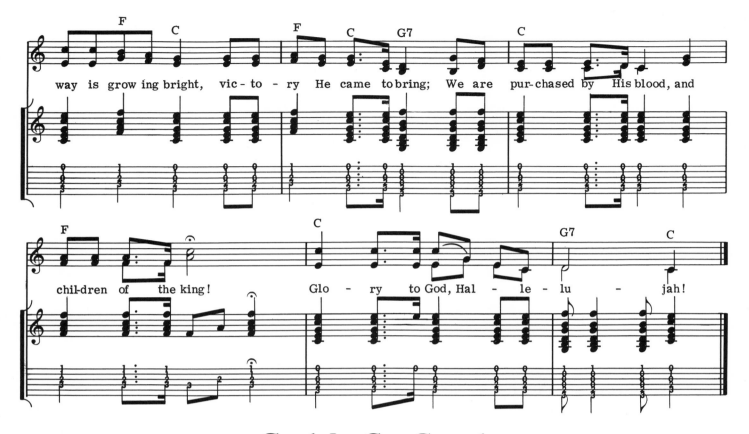

way is grow ing bright, vic - to - ry He came to bring; We are pur-chased by His blood, and

chil-dren of the king! Glo - ry to God, Hal - le - lu - jah!

God Is So Good

1. God is so good, God is so good,
2. God cares for me
3. I'll trust in Him
4. Je - sus is Lord

God is so good, He's so good to me.

5. I'll sing His praise.

Amazing Grace

John Newton
1725-1807

Early American Melody

1. A - maz - ing grace! How sweet the sound, That
2. 'Twas grace that taught My heart to fear, And
3. 'Thru man - y, dan - gers, toils and snares, I
4. When we've been there ten thou - sand years, Bright

saved a wretch like me! I
grace my fears re - lieved; How
have al - read - y come; 'Tis
shin - ing as the sun, We've

once was lost but now am found, Was
pre - cious did that grace ap - pear, The
grace hath brought me safe thus far, And
no less days to sing God's praise Than

blind, but now I see.
hour I first be - lieved!
grace will lead me home.
when we first be - gun. A - men.

5. Alleluia, Alleluia, Alleluia, Praise God! (Repeat)

20

Jesus Is His Name

Bill Bay

I Will Praise Him

Margaret J. Harris
19th Cent.

1. When I saw the cleans-ing foun-tain O - pen wide for all my sin,
2. Then God's fire up-on the al-tar Of my heart was set a - flame;
3. Glo - ry, glo - ry to the Fa - ther! Glo - ry, glo - ry to the Son!

I o - beyed the Spir - it's woo - ing, When He said, "Wilt thou be clean?"
I shall nev - er cease to praise Him, Glo - ry, glo - ry to His name!
Glo - ry, glo - ry to the Spir - it! Glo - ry to the Three in One!

Chorus

I will praise Him! I will praise Him! Praise the Lamb for sin-ners slain:

Give Him glo - ry, all ye peo - ple, For His blood can wash a-way each stain.

Behold The Glories Of The Lamb

Verses Isaac Watts
Chorus Wm. Bay

Wm. Bay

1. Be-hold the glo - ries of the Lamb, A - mid His Fa - ther's throne; Pre-
2. Let el - ders wor - ship at His feet, The chruch a - dore a - round, With
3. Now to the Lamb that once was slain, Be end - less bless - ings paid! Sal -
4. Thou hast re-deemed our souls with blood, Hast set the pri - soners free; Hast

pare new hon - ors for His name, And songs be - fore un - known.
vi - als full of o - dors sweet, And harps of sweet - er sound.
va - tion, glo - ry, joy re - main For - ev - er on Thy head.
made us kings and priests to God, And we shall reign with Thee.

Chorus

Em - man - u - el, We lift up our hearts and we sing, Em -

man - u - el, Our Lord, our Re-deem - er, and King!

Precious Name

Lydia Baxter
1809-1874

William H. Doane
1832-1915

1. Take the name of Je - sus with you, Child of sor - row and of woe;
2. Take the name of Je - sus ev - er, As a shield from ev - 'ry snare;
3. O the pre-cious name of Je - sus! How it thrills our souls with joy,

It will joy and com-fort give you; Take it, then, wher e'er you go.
If temp-ta-tion round you gath - er, Breathe that ho - ly name in prayer.
When His lov-ing arms re - ceive us, And His songs our tongues em-ploy!

Refrain

Pre-cious name, O how sweet! Hope of earth and joy of heav'n; Pre-cious

name, O how sweet! Hope of earth and joy of heav'n. A - men.

Mine Eyes And My Desire

Unto You, Lord

Bill Bay

Allelu, Praise The Lord

By Bill Bay

Blessed Assurance

Fanny Crosby
1820-1915

Phoebe Knapp
1839-1908

1. Bless-ed as - sur - ance, Je - sus is mine! O what a
2. Per-fect sub - mis - sion, per-fect de - light, Vi - sions of
3. Per-fect sub - mis - sion, all is at rest; I in my

fore - taste of glo - ry di - vine! Heir of sal -
rap - ture now burst on my sight; An - gels de -
Sav - ior am hap - py and blest, Watch-ing and

va - tion, pur - chase of God, Born of His
scend - ing, bring from a - bove Ech - oes of
wait - ing, look - ing a - bove Filled with His

Spir - it, washed in His blood. This is my
mer - cy, whis - pers of love.
good - ness, lost in His love.

sto - ry, this is my song, Prais - ing my

Sav - ior all the day long, This is my

sto - ry, this is my song, Prais-ing my

Sav - ior all the day long. A - men.

Have Thine Own Way, Lord

Adelaide
A. Pollard, 1902

George
C. Stebbins, 1907

Have Thine own way, Lord! Have Thine own way!

1. Thou art the pot - ter, I am the clay.
2. Search me and try me, Mas - ter, to - day!
3. Wound - ed and wea - ry, help me, I pray!
4. Hold o'er my be - ing, ab - so - lute sway!

Mold me and make me af - ter Thy will,
Whit - er than snow, Lord, wash me just now,
Pow - er all pow - er sure - ly is Thine!
Fill with Thy Spir - it till all shall see

While I am wait - ing yield-ed and still.
As in Thy Pres - ence hum-bly I bow.
Touch me and heal me, Sav - ior di - vine.
Christ on - ly, al - ways, liv -ing in me!

Old Rugged Cross

George
Bennard 1913

Softly And Tenderly

Will L. Thompson
1847-1909

Slowly

1. Soft - ly and ten - der - ly Je - sus is call - ing,
2. Why should we tar - ry when Je - sus is plead - ing,
3. Time is now fleet - ing, the mo - ments are pass - ing,
4. O for the won - der - ful love He has prom - ised,

Call - ing for you and for me;
Plead - ing for you and for me?
Pass - ing from you and from me;
Prom - ised for you and for me;

See, on the por - tals He's wait - ing and watch - ing,
Why should we lin - ger and heed not His mer - cies,
Sha - dows are gath - er - ing death beds are com - ing,
Tho we have sinned He has mer - cy and par - don,

Watch - ing for you and for me.
Mer - cies for you and for me.
Com - ing for you and for me.
Par - don for you and for me.

Chorus

Come home, come home, Ye who are wea-ry, come

home; Earn - est - ly, ten - der - ly,

Je - sus is call - ing Call - ing," O sin - ner, come

home!" A - men.

Almost Persuaded

Phillip P. Bliss
1838-1876

Lord, I'm Coming Home

William J. Kirkpatrick
1838-1921

1. I've wan - dered far a - way___ from God, Now I'm com-ing home; The paths of sin too long I've trod, Lord, I'm com-ing home.
2. I've wast - ed man - y pre - cious years, Now I'm com-ing home; I now re-pent with bit - ter tears, Lord, I'm com-ing home.
3. I've tired of sin and stray - ing, Lord, Now I'm com-ing home; I'll trust Thy love, be - lieve Thy word, Lord, I'm com-ing home.
4. My soul is sick, my heart___ is sore, Now I'm com-ing home; My strength re-new, my hope re-store, Lord, I'm com-ing home.

Chorus

Com-ing home, com-ing home, Nev - er -more to roam, O - pen wide Thine arms of love, Lord, I'm com-ing home.___ A - men.

Every Day and Every Hour

Fanny J. Crosby
1820-1915

William H. Doane
1832-1915

1. Sav-ior, more than life to me, I am cling-ing, cling-ing close to Thee; Let Thy
2. Thru this chang - ing world be-low, Lead me gent - ly, gent - ly as I go; Trust-ing
3. Let me love Thee more and more, Till this fleet-ing, fleet-ing life is o'er; Till my

pre - cious blood ap-plied, Keep me ev - er, ev - er near Thy side.
Thee, I can - not stray; I can nev - er, nev - er lose my way.
soul is lost in love, In a bright- er, bright-er world a - bove.

Refrain

Ev - 'ry day, ev-'ry hour, Let me feel Thy cleans-ing pow'r; May Thy ten - der love to me Bind me closer, clos-er, Lord, to Thee. A - men.

Near The Cross

Fanny J. Crosby
1820-1915

William H. Doane
1832-1915

1. Je - sus keep me near the cross, There a pre - cious foun - tain;
2. Near the cross, a trem-bling soul, Love and mer - cy found me;
3. Near the cross! O Lamb of God, Bring its scenes be - fore me;

Free to all, a heal - ing stream, Flows from Cal - viny's moun - tain.
There the bright and morn - ing star Shed its beams a - round me.
Help me walk from day to day With its shad - ow o'er me.

Refrain

In the cross, in the cross, Be my glo - ry ev - er,

Till my rap-tured soul shall find Rest be-yond the riv - er. A - men.

Just As I Am

Charlotte Elliott
1789-1871

Wm Bradbury
1816-1868

1. Just as I am, with-out one plea, But that Thy blood was
2. Just as I am, and wait-ing not To rid my soul of
3. Just as I am, tho tossed a-bout With man-y a con - flict,
4. Just as I am, Thou wilt re-ceive, Wilt wel - come, par - don,

shed for me, And that Thou bidd'st me come to Thee
one dark blot, To Thee whose blood can cleanse each spot
many a doubt, Fight - ings and fears with - in, with - out O
cleanse, re - lieve, Be - cause Thy prom - ise I be - lieve,

Lamb of God, I come! I

come! A - men.

He Leadeth Me!

Joseph H. Gilmore
1834-1918

William B. Bradbury
1816-1868

1. He lead-eth me! O bless-ed tho't O words with hea-ven-ly com-fort fraught! What e'er I do, where-e'er I be, Still 'tis God's hand that lead-eth me!

2. Some-times 'mid scenes of deep-est gloom, Some-times where E-den's bow-ers bloom, By wa-ters still, o'er trou-bled sea, Still 'tis His hand that lead-eth me! He

3. Lord, I would clasp Thy hand in mine, Nor ev-er mur-mur nor re-pine, Con-tent, what-ev-er lot I see, Since 'tis Thy hand that lead-eth me!

Refrain

He lead-eth me, He lead-eth me, By His own hand He lead-eth me: His faith-ful fol-l'wer I would be, For by His hand He lead-eth me. A-men.

Revive Us Again

William P. Mackay
1839-1885

John J. Husband
1760-1825

1. We praise Thee, O God, for the Son of Thy love, For
2. We praise Thee, O God, for Thy Spir - it of light, Who has
3. All glo - ry and praise to the Lamb that was slain, Who has

Je - sus who died and is now gone a - bove.
shown us our Sav - ior and scat - tered our night.
borne all our sins and has cleansed ev - 'ry stain.

Chorus

Hal - le - lu - jah, Thine the glo - ry! Hal - le - lu - jah, a - men! Hal - le - lu - jah, Thine the glo - ry! Re - vive us a - gain.

A - men.

Jesus, I Come

William T. Sleeper
1819-1904

George C. Stebbins
1846-1945

1. Out of my bond-age, sor-row and night, Je-sus, I come, Je-sus, I come;
2. Out of my shame-ful fail-ure and loss, Je-sus, I come, Je-sus, I come;
3. Out of un-rest and ar-ro-gant pride, Je-sus, I come, Je-sus, I come;

In - to Thy free-dom, glad-ness and light, Je-sus, I come to Thee.
In - to The glo-rious gain of Thy cross, Je-sus, I come to Thee.
In - to Thy bless-ed will to a-bide, Je-sus, I come to Thee.

Out of my sick-ness in - to Thy health, Out of my want and in - to Thy wealth,
Out of earth's sor-row in - to Thy balm, Out of life's storms and in - to Thy calm
Out of my-self to dwell in Thy love, Out of de-spair into rap-tures a-bove,

Out of my sin and in - to Thy-self,
Out of dis-tress to ju-bi-lant psalm, Je-sus, I come to Thee. A - men.
Up-ward for aye on wings like a dove,

Just A Closer Walk

Slowly

Source Unknown

I Am Resolved

Palmer Hartsough
1844-1932

James H. Fillmore
1849-1936

1. I am re-solved no lon-ger to lin-ger, Charmed by the world's de-light;
2. I am re-solved to fol-low the Sav-ior, Faith-ful and true each day;
3. I am re-solved to en-ter the king-dom, leav-ing the paths of sin;
4. I am re-solved, and who will go with me? Come, friends with-out de-lay,

Things that are high-er, things that are no-bler, These have al-lured my sight.
Heed what He say-eth, do what He will-eth, He is the liv-ing way.
Friends may ap-pose me, foes may be-set me, Still I will en-ter in.
Taught by the Bi-ble, led by the Spir-it, We'll walk the heav'n-ly way.

Refrain

I will has-ten to Him, Has-ten so glad and free,

Je - sus, great-est, high-est, I will come to Thee! A - men.

Whiter Than Snow

James L. Nicholson
C. 1828-1876

William G. Fischer
1835-1912

1. Lord Je - sus, I long to be per - fect - ly whole; I want Thee for -
2. Lord Je - sus, look down from Thy throne in the skies, And help me to
3. Lord Je - sus, for this I most hum - bly en - treat; I wait, bless-ed

ev - er to live in my soul; Break down ev - 'ry i - dol, cast
make a com - plete sac - ri - fice; I give up my - self and what -
Lord, at Thy cru - ci - fied feet; By faith, for my cleans - ing I

out ev - 'ry foe: Now wash me, and I shall be whit - er than snow.
ev - er I know: Now wash me, and I shall be whit - er than snow.
see Thy blood flow: Now wash me, and I shall be whit - er than snow.

Refrain

Whit - er than snow, yes, whit - er than snow; Now wash me, and

44

Close To Thee

Fanny J. Crosby
1820-1915

Silas J. Vail
1818-1884

1. Thou, my ev - er-last-ing por - tion, More than friend or life to me; All a-
2. Not for ease or world-ly pleas-ure, Nor for fame my pray'r shall be; Glad-ly
3. Lead me thru the vale of shad-ows, Bear me o'er life's fit - ful sea; Then the

long my pil-grim jour-ney, Sav - ior, let me walk with Thee. Close to Thee, close to Thee, Close to
will I toil and suf-fer, On - ly let me walk with Thee. Close to Thee, close to Thee, Close to
gate of life e - ter-nal May I en - ter, Lord, with Thee. Close to Thee, close to Thee, Close to

Refrain

Thee, close to Thee; All a-long my pil-grim jour-ney, Sav-ior, let me walk with Thee.
Thee, close to Thee; Glad-ly will I toil and suf-fer, On-ly let me walk with Thee.
Thee, close to Thee; Then the gate of life e - ter-nal May I en-ter, Lord, with Thee. A - men.

All For Jesus

Mary D. James, 1889

Source Unknown

1. All for Je - sus, all for Je - sus! All my be - ing's ran-somed
2. Let my hands per-form His bid - ding, Let my feet run in His
3. Since my eyes were fixed on Je - sus, I've lost sight of all be -
4. Oh, what won - der! how a - maz - ing! Je - sus, glo - rious King of

pow'rs: All my thoughts and words and do - ings,
ways; Let my eyes see Je - sus on - ly,
side; So en - chained my spir - it's vi - sion,
kings, Deigns to call me His be - lov - ed,

All my days and all my hours. All for Je-sus! all for Je - sus!
Let my lips speak forth His praise.
Look - ing at the Cru - ci - fied.
Lets me rest be - neath His wings.

All my days and all my hours; hours.
Let my lips speak forth His praise; praise.
Look - ing at the Cru - ci - fied; fied.
Rest - ing now be - neath His wings; wings.

Tis So Sweet

Louisa M. R. Stead
c. 1850-1917

William J. Kirkpatrick
1838-1921

1. 'Tis so sweet to trust in Je - sus, And to take Him at His word;
2. O how sweet to trust in Je - sus, Just to trust His cleans-ing blood;
3. Yes 'tis sweet to trust in Je - sus, Just from sin and self to cease;

Just to rest up - on His prom-ise, And to know, "Thus saith the Lord."
And in sim - ple faith to plunge me Neath the heal - ing, cleans-ing flood!
Just from Je - sus sim - ply tak - ing Life and rest, and joy and peace.

Refrain

Je - sus, Je - sus, how I trust Him! How I've proved Him o'er and o'er!

Je - sus, Je - sus, pre - cious Je - sus! O for grace to trust Him more! A - men.

I Surrender All

Judson W. Van de Venter
1855-1939

Winfield S. Weeden
1847-1908

1. All to Jesus I surrender, All to Him I freely give;
2. All to Jesus I surrender, Humbly at His feet I bow,
3. All to Jesus I surrender, Make me, Savior, wholly Thine;
4. All to Jesus I surrender, Lord, I give myself to Thee;

I will ever love and trust Him, In His presence daily live.
Worldly pleasures all forsaken, take me, Jesus take me now.
Let me feel the Holy Spirit, truly know that Thou art mine.
Fill me with Thy love and power, let Thy blessing fall on me.

Chorus

I surrender all, I surrender all,

All to Thee, my blessed Savior, I surrender all,

Look To The Lamb of God

H. G. Jackson

James M. Black
1856-1938

1. If you from sin are long - ing to be free, Look to the Lamb of God;
2. When Sa-tan tempts, and doubts and fears as - sail, Look to the Lamb of God;
3. Fear not when shad - ows on your path-way fall, Look to the Lamb of God;

He, to re-deem you, died on Cal-va - ry, Look to the Lamb of God.
You in His strength shall o - ver all pre-vail, Look to the Lamb of God.
In joy or sor - row Christ is all in all Look to the Lamb of God.

Chorus

Look to the Lamb of God, Look to the Lamb of God,

For He alone is a - ble to save you; Look to the Lamb of God.

Jesus, Savior, Pilot Me

Edward Hopper
1816-1888

John E. Gould
1822-1875

1. Je-sus, Sav-ior, pi-lot me Over life's tem-pes-tuous sea; Un-known
2. As a moth-er stills her child, Thou canst hush the o-cean wild; Bois-t'rous
3. When at last I near the shore, And the fear-ful break-ers roar 'Twixt me

waves be-fore me roll, Hid-ing rock and treach-'rous shoal; Chart and
waves o-bey Thy will When Thou sayest to them, "Be still!" Won-drous
waves and the peace-ful rest, Then, while lean-ing on Thy breast, May I

com-pass came from Thee: Je-sus, Sav-ior, pi-lot me.
sov-ereign of the sea, Je-sus, Sav-ior, pi-lot me.
hear Thee say to me, "Fear not, I will pi-lot Thee." A - men.

I'll Live For Him

Ralph E. Hudson
1843-1901

C. R. Dunbar

1. My life, my love, I give to thee, Thou Lamb of God, who died for me; Oh,
2. O Thou who died on Cal-va-ry, To save my soul and make me free, I'll
3. I'll live for Him who died for me, How hap-py then my life shall be! I'll

Lonesome Valley

Spiritual

Send The Light

Charles H. Gabriel
1856-1932

1. There's a call comes ring-ing o'er the rest-less wave, "Send the light! Send the
2. Let us pray that grace may ev-'ry-where a - bound, Send the light! Send the
3. Let us not grow wea-ry in the work of love, Send the light! Send the

light!" There are souls to res-cue, there are souls to save, Send the light! Send the
light! And the Ho - ly Spir-it ev-'ry-where be found, Send the light! Send the
light! Let us gath - er jew-els for a crown a - bove, Send the light! Send the

Refrain

light!
light!
light!

Send the light! The bless-ed gos-pel light; Let it shine from shore to

shore! Send the light! The bless-ed gos-pel light; Let it shine for ev-er-more.

Give Me Jesus

Fanny J. Crosby
1820-1915

John R. Sweney
1837-1899

1. Take the world, but give me Je - sus All its joys are but a name; But His
2. Take the world, but give me Je - sus Let me view His con - stant smile; Then thru
3. Take the world, but give me Je - sus In His cross my trust shall be; Till, with

love a - bid - eth ev - er, Thru e - ter - nal years the same.
out my pil - grim jour - ney, Light will cheer me all the while.
clear - er, bright - er vi - sion, Face to face my Lord I see.

Chorus

O the height and depth of mer - cy! O the length and breadth of love! O the

full - ness of re - demp - tion Pledge of end - less life a - bove.

Tis Burning In My Soul

Delia T. White
19th Century

William J. Kirkpatrick
1838-1921

1. God sent His might-y pow'r To this poor, sin-ful heart, To keep me ev-'ry hour, And
2. Be-fore the cross I bow, Up - on the al - tar lay A will-ing of-fring now, My
3. No good that I have done, His prom-ise I em-brace; Ac-cept-ed in the Son, He

need-ful grace im-part; And since His Spir-it came, To take su-preme con-trol, The
all from day to day. My Sav - ior paid the price, My name He sweet-ly calls; Up-
saves me by His grace. All glo - ry be to God! Let hal - le - lu - jahs roll; His

love en - kin-dled flame Is burn-ing in my soul.
on the sac - ri - fice The fire from heav - en falls.   'Tis burn-ing in my soul,   'Tis
love is shed a-broad, The fire is in my soul

Chorus

burn-ing in my soul; The fire of heav'n-ly love is burn-ing in my soul   The Ho-ly Spir - it came, All

glo-ry to His name. The fire of Heav'n-ly love is burn-ing in my soul.

More Love To Thee

Elisabeth P. Prentiss
1818-1878

William H. Doane
1832-1915

1. More love to Thee, O Christ, More love to Thee! Hear Thou the
2. Once earth-ly joy I craved, Sought peace and rest; Now Thee a -
3. Then shall my lat - est breath Whis - per Thy praise; This be the

prayer I make, On bend-ed knee; This is my earn - est plea; More love, O
lone I seek, Give what is best. This all my prayer shall be: More love, O
part - ing cry My heart shall raise: This still its prayer shall be, More love, O

Christ, to Thee, More love to Thee, More love to Thee!
Christ, to Thee, More love to Thee, More love to Thee!
Christ, to Thee, More love to Thee, More love to Thee! A - Men.

Every Bridge Is Burned Behind Me

Rev. Johnson
Oatman, Jr

Geo. L. Hugg, 1898

1. Since I start-ed out to find Thee, Since I to the cross did flee,
2. Thou didst hear my plea so kind-ly, Thou didst grant me so much grace;
3. All in all, I ev - er find Thee, Sav - ior, Lov - er Bro - ther, Friend;

Ev - 'ry bridge is burned be-hind me, I will nev - er turn from Thee.
Ev - 'ry bridge is burned be-hind me, I will ne'er my steps re-trace.
Ev - 'ry bridge is burned be-hind me, I will serve Thee to the end.

Chorus

Strength - en all the ties that bind me Clos - er, clos - er, Lord, to Thee;

Ev - 'ry bridge is burned be-hind me, Thine I ev - er - more will be.

I Am Coming, Lord

Lewis Hartsough
1828-1919

1. I hear Thy wel-come voice, that calls me, Lord, to Thee, For
2. 'Tis Je - sus calls me on to per - fect faith and love, To

cleans - ing in Thy pre-cious blood That flowed on Cal - va - ry.
per - fect hope, and peace and trust, For earth and heav'n a - bove.

Chorus

I am com-ing, Lord! Com - ing now to Thee!

Wash me, cleanse me in the blood That flowed on Cal - va - ry!

Follow On

William O. Cushing
1823-1902

Robert Lowry
1826-1899

1. Down in the val-ley with my Sav-ior I would go, Where the flowers are bloom-ing and the
2. Down in the val-ley with my Sav-ior I would go, Where the storms are sweep-ing and the
3. Down in the val-ley, or up-on the moun-tain steep Close be-side my Sav-ior would my

sweet wa-ters flow;   Ev-'ry-where He leads me I would fol-low, fol-low on,
dark wa-ters flow;   With His hand to lead me I will nev-er, nev-er fear,
soul ev-er keep;   He will lead me safe-ly in the path that He has trod,

Chorus

Walk-ing in His foot steps till the crown be won.   Fol-low! fol-low!
Dan-ger can-not fright me if my Lord is near.
Up to where they gath-er on the hills of God.

I would fol-low Je-sus! An-y-where, ev-'ry-where, I would fol-low on!

Jesus Calls Us

Cecil F. Alexander
1818-1895

William H. Jude
1851-1922

Ev - 'ry - where He leads me I would fol - low on!

1. Je - sus calls us o'er the tu - mult Of our life's wild, rest - less
2. Je - sus calls us from the wor - ship Of the vain world's gold - en
3. In - our joys and in our sor - rows, Days of toil and hours of
4. Je - sus calls us: by Thy mer - cies, Sav-ior, may we hear Thy

sea; Day by day His sweet voice sound - eth, Say - ing,
store, From each i - dol that would keep us, Say - ing,
ease, Still He calls, in cares and pleas - ures, "Christ - ian,
call, Give our hearts to Thy o - be - dience, Serve and

"Chris - tian, fol - low me."
"Chris - tian, love me more."
love Me more than these."
love Thee best of all.   A - - men.

Channels Only

Mary E. Maxwell

Ada Rose Gibbs
1865-1905

1. How I praise Thee, pre-cious Sav - ior, That Thy love laid hold of me; Thou hast
2. Emp-tied that Thou should-est fill me, A clean ves - sel in Thy hand; With no
3. Je - sus, fill now with Thy Spir - it Hearts that full sur - ren - der know; That the

saved and cleansed and filled me That I might Thy chan-nel be.
power but as Thou giv - est Gra-cious - ly with each com - mand.
streams of liv - ing wa - ter From our in - ner man may flow.

Chorus

Chan-nels

on - ly, bless-ed Mas - ter, But with all Thy won-drous pow'r Flow-ing

thru us, Thou canst use us Ev-'ry day and ev - 'ry hour.

Holy Spirit, Dwell In Me

Bill Bay

All The Way My Savior Leads Me

Fanny J. Crosby
1820-1915

Robert Lowry
1826-1899

Where He Leads Me

E. W. Blandy
19th Century

J. S. Norris
1844-1907

Is Your All On The Altar

Elisha A. Hoffman
1839-1929

1. You have longed for sweet peace, and for faith to in - crease, And have
2. Would you walk with the Lord in the light of His Word, And have
3. Who can tell all the love He will send from a - bove, And how

ear - nest-ly, fer - vent-ly prayed; But you
peace and con - tent - ment al - way, You must
hap - py our hearts will be made, Of the

can - not have rest or be per - fect-ly blest Un - til
do His sweet will to be free from all ill, On the
fel - low-ship sweet we shall share at His feet, When our

all on the al - tar is laid.
al - tar your all you must lay.
all on the al - tar is laid.

I Love To Tell The Story

Katherine Hankey,
1834-1911

William G. Fischer,
1835-1912

At The Cross

Isaac Watts 1674-1748
Chorus-Ralph E. Hudson

Ralph E. Hudson
1843-1901

1. A - las! and did my Sav - ior bleed? And did my Sov - 'reign die? Would He de-vote that sa - cred head For such a soul as I?
2. Was it for crimes that I have done He groaned up - on the tree? A - maz - ing pit - y! grace un known! And love be - yond de - gree!
3. Well might the sun in dark - ness hide And shut his glo - ries in, When Christ, the might - y Mak - er, died For man the crea - ture's sin.
4. But drops of grief can ne'er re - pay The debt of love I owe: Here, Lord, I give my - self a - way 'Tis all that I can do!

Chorus

At the cross, at the cross where I first saw the light, And the bur-den of my heart rolled a-way It was there by faith I re-ceived my sight, And now I am hap-py all the day! A - men.

Standing On The Promises

R. Kelso Carter
1849-1926

1. Stand-ing on the prom-is-es of Christ my King, Thru e-ter-nal a - ges let His prais-es ring;
2. Stand-ing on the prom-is-es that can - not fail, When the howl-ing storms of doubt and fear as - sail,
3. Stand-ing on the prom-is-es of Christ the Lord, Bound to Him e - ter - nal-ly by love's strong cord,

Glo - ry in the high-est I will shout and sing, Stand-ing on the prom-is - es of God.
By the liv-ing Word of God I shall pre-vail, Stand-ing on the prom-is - es of God.
O - ver com-ing dai - ly with the Spir-it's sword, Stand-ing on the prom-is - es of God.

Refrain

Stand - ing, stand - ing, Stand-ing on the prom-is-es of God my Sav - ior;

Stand - ing, stand - ing, I'm stand-ing on the prom-is-es of God. A - men.

Nothing But The Blood

Robert Lowry
1826-1899

1. What can wash a - way my sin? Noth - ing but the blood of Je - sus;
2. For my par - don this I see. Noth - ing but the blood of Je - sus;
3. This is all my hope and peace. Noth - ing but the blood of Je - sus;

What can make me whole a - gain? Noth - ing but the blood of Je - sus.
For my cleans - ing, this my plea. Noth - ing but the blood of Je - sus.
This is all my right-eous-ness. Noth - ing but the blood of Je - sus.

Refrain

Oh! pre - cious is the flow That makes me white as snow;

No oth - er fount I know, Noth - ing but the blood of Je - sus!

A Glorious Church

Ralph E. Hudson
1843-1901

1. Do you hear them com - ing, broth - er, Throng-ing up the streams of light,
2. Do you hear the stir - ring an - thems, Fill - ing all the earth and sky,
3. Nev - er fear the clouds of sor - row, Nev - er fear the storms of sin,

Clad in glo - rious shin-ing gar-ments, Blood washed gar-ments pure and white?
'Tis a grand, vic - to - rious ar - my, Lift its ban - ner up on high!
We shall tri - umph on the mor-row, E - ven now our joys be - gin.

Chorus

'Tis a glo - rious church with - out spot or wrin-kle, Washed in the blood of the lamb; 'Tis a

glo - rious church, with - out spot or wrin-kle, Washed in the blood of the lamb.

70

Jesus Paid It All

Elvina M. Hall
1820-1889

John T. Grape
1835-1915

1. I hear the Sav-ior say, "Thy strength in-deed is small, Child of
2. Lord, now in-deed I find Thy pow'r and Thine a-lone, Can
3. And when, before the throne, I stand in Him com-plete, "Je-sus

weak-ness, watch and pray, Find in me Thine all in all."
change the lep-er's spots, And melt the heart of stone.
died my soul to save," My lips shall still re-peat.

Je-sus paid it all, All to Him I owe; Sin had left a

crim-son stain, He washed it white as snow.

The Hallelujah Side

Johnson Oatman, Jr.
1856-1922

J. Howard Entwisle

1. Once a sin - ner far from Je - sus, I was per - ish - ing with cold, But the
2. Tho' the world may sweep a - round me with her daz - zle and her dreams, Yet I
3. Not for all earth's gol - den mil - lions would I leave this pre - cious place, Tho' the
4. Here the sun is al - ways shin - ing, here the sky is al - ways bright; 'Tis no

bless - ed Sav - ior heard me when I cried; Then He threw His robe a - round me, and He
en - vy not her van - i - ties and pride, For my soul looks up to Heav - en, where the
tempt - er to per - suade me oft has tried, For I'm safe in God's pa - vil - ion, hap - py
place for gloom - y Christ - ians to a - bide, For my soul is filled with mu - sic and my

led me to His fold, And I'm liv - ing on the hal - le - lu - jah side.
gold - en sun - light gleams,
in His love and grace,
heart with great de - light,

Oh,

glo -'ry be to Je - sus, let the hal - le - lu - jahs roll; Help me ring the Sav - ior's prais - es far and wide, For I've

72

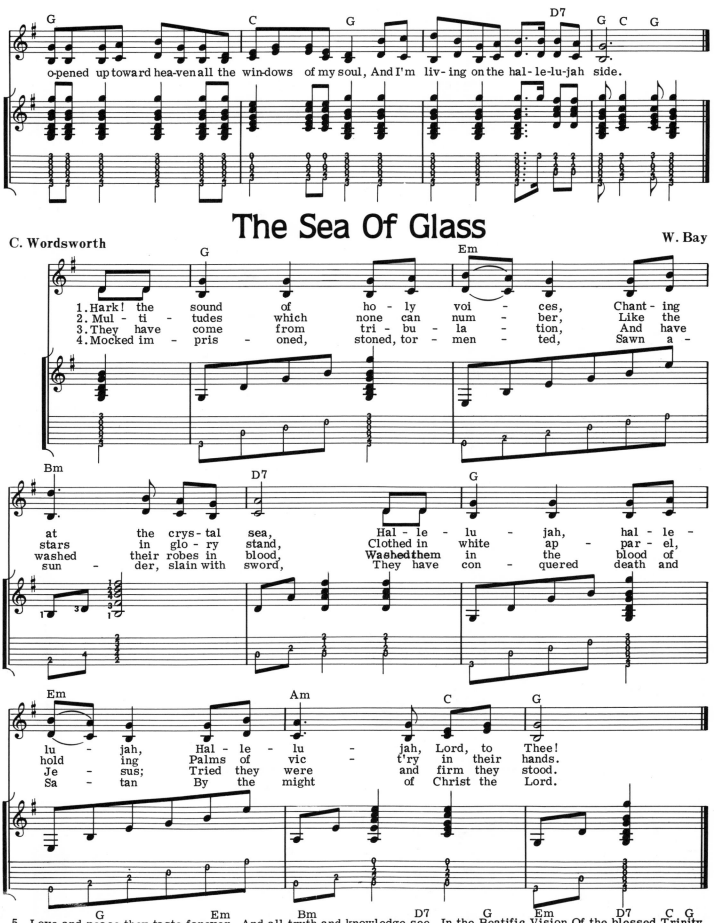

The Sea Of Glass

C. Wordsworth

W. Bay

o-pened up toward hea-ven all the win-dows of my soul, And I'm liv-ing on the hal-le-lu-jah side.

1. Hark! the sound of ho-ly voi - ces, Chant - ing at the crys-tal sea, Hal - le - lu - jah, hal-le-lu - jah, Hal-le-lu - jah, Lord, to Thee!
2. Mul - ti - tudes which none can num - ber, Like the stars in glo - ry stand, Clothed in white ap - par - el, hold - ing Palms of vic - t'ry in their hands.
3. They have come from tri-bu-la - tion, And have washed their robes in blood, Washed them in the blood of Je - sus; Tried they were and firm they stood.
4. Mocked im - pris - oned, stoned, tor - men - ted, Sawn a - sun - der, slain with sword, They have con - quered death and Sa - tan By the might of Christ the Lord.

5. Love and peace they taste forever, And all truth and knowledge see, In the Beatific Vision Of the blessed Trinity.

Death Has No Terrors

C. P. Jones

1. Death has no ter-rors for the blood bought one, O glo-ry hal-le-lu-jah to the Lamb! The
2. Our souls die dai-ly to the world and sin, O glo-ry hal-le-lu-jah to the Lamb! By the
3. We'll then press for-ward to the heav'n-ly land, Vic-t'ry

boast-ed vic-t'ry of the grave is gone, O glo-ry hal-le-lu-jah to the Lamb!
Spir-it's pow-er as He dwells with-in,
o'er the trou-bles met on ev-'ry hand,

Chorus

Je-sus rose from the dead, Rose tri-um - phant as He said, Snatched the

vic-t'ry from the grave, Rose a-gain our souls to save O glo-ry hal-le-lu-jah to the Lamb!

Higher Ground

Johnson Oatman, Jr.
1856-1922

Chas. H. Gabriel
1856-1932

1. I'm press-ing on the up-ward way, New heights I'm gain-ing ev-'ry-day; Still pray-ing
2. I want to live a-bove the world, Tho' Sa-tan's darts at me are hurled; For faith has
3. I want to scale the ut-most height, And catch a gleam of glo-ry bright; But still I'll

as I on-ward bound, "Lord, plant my feet on high-er ground."
caught the joy-ful sound, The song of saints on high-er ground.
pray, till heav'n I've found, "Lord, lead me on to high-er ground."

Lord, lift me up and let me stand, By faith, on heav-en's ta-ble-land; A high-er plane than I have found Lord, plant my feet on high-er ground. A - men.

The Lord Is My Shepherd
(PSALM 23)

by Bill Bay

Moderately

pre - sence of mine en - e - mies: Thou a - noint-est my

head with oil; my cup run-neth o - ver.

Sure - ly good-ness and mer - cy shall fol-low me all the

days of my life: and I will dwell

in the house of the Lord for - ev - -

er; for - ev - er.

Guitar Accompaniment

Peace I Give You

Bill Bay

Leaning On The Everlasting Arms

Elisha A. Hoffman
1839-1929

Anthony J. Showalter
1858-1924

Precious Memories

J.B.F. Wright
Vs 4-W. Bay

J.B.F. Wright

I Need Thee Every Hour

Annie S. Hawks
1835-1918

Robert Lowry
1826-1899

The Solid Rock

Edward Mote
1797-1874

William B. Bradbury
1816-1868

1. My hope is built on noth-ing less Than Je - sus' blood and
2. His oath, His cov - e - nant, His blood Sup - port me in the
3. When He shall come with trum-pet sound, Oh, may I then in

right-eous-ness; I dare not trust the sweet-est frame, But whol-ly lean on
whelm-ing flood; When all a-round my soul gives way, He then is all my
Him be found; Dressed in His right - eous - ness a - lone, Fault - less to stand be -

Refrain

Je - sus' name.
hope and stay. On Christ, the sol - id Rock, I stand; All oth - er ground is
fore the throne.

sink-ing sand, All oth - er ground is sink-ing sand. A - men.

Only Trust Him

John H. Stockton
1813-1877

1. Come, ev - 'ry soul by sin op-pressed, There's mer - cy with the Lord; And
2. For Je - sus shed His pre - cious blood Rich bless-ings to be - stow; Plunge
3. Yes, Je - sus is the truth, the way, That leads you in - to rest; Be -
4. Come then and join this ho - ly band, And on to glo - ry go, To

He will sure - ly give you rest, By trust - ing in His word.
now in - to the crim - son flood That wash - es white as snow.
lieve in Him with - out de - lay, And you are ful - ly blest.
dwell in that ce - les - tial land, Where joys im-mor - tal flow.

On - ly trust Him, On - ly trust Him, On - ly trust Him now;

He will save you, He will save you, He will save you now. A - men.

Rock Of Ages

Augustus M. Toplady
1740-1778

Thomas Hastings
1784-1872

1. Rock of A - ges, cleft for me, Let me hide my - self in thee', Let the wa - ter and the blood, From Thy wound - ed side which flowed, Be of sin the dou - ble cure, Save from wrath and make me pure.

2. Could my tears for - ev - er flow, Could my zeal no lan - guor know, These for sin could not a - tone; Thou must save, and Thou a - lone. In my hand no price I bring; Sim - ply to Thy cross I cling.

3. While I draw this fleet - ing breath, When my eyes shall close in death, When I rise to worlds un - known, And be - hold Thee on Thy throne, Rock of A - ges, cleft for me, Let me hide my - self in Thee. A - men.

What A Friend We Have In Jesus

Joseph Scriven
1832-1918

Charles C. Converse
1819-1886

1. What a friend we have in Je - sus All our sins and griefs to bear!
2. Have we trials - and temp - ta - tions? Is there trou-ble an-y-where?
3. Are we weak and heav-y la - den, Cum - bered with a load of care?

What a priv - i-lege to car - ry ev - 'ry-thing to God in prayer!____
We should nev-er be dis-cour - aged, Take it to the Lord in prayer!____
Pre - cious Sa-vior, still or re - fuge, Take it to the Lord in prayer!____

O what peace we of - ten for - feit, O what need-less pain we bear,
Can we find a friend so faith - ful Who will all our sor-rows share?
Do thy friends de-spise, for sake thee? Take it to the Lord in prayer,

All be-cause we do not car - ry Ev - 'ry-thing to Good in prayer!
Je - sus knows our ev - 'ry weak - ness Take it to the Lord in prayer!
In His arms He'll take and shield thee, Thou wilt find a sol-ace there. A - men.

I'm A Child Of The King

Hattie E. Buell

Peace, Perfect Peace

Edward H. Bickersteth
1825-1906

Orlando Gibbons
1583-1625

1. Peace, per - fect peace, in this dark world of sin? The
2. Peace, per - fect peace, by throng - ing du - ties pressed? To
3. Peace, per - fect peace, with sor - rows sur - ging round? On
4. Peace, per - fect peace, with our fu - ture all un - known? Je -

blood of Je - sus whis - pers peace with - in.
do the will of Je - sus: this is rest.
Je - sus' bos - om nought but calm is found.
sus we know, and He is on the throne! A - men.

Never Alone

Chorus is sung
after each verse

Source Unknown

Near To The Heart Of God

Cleland B. McAfee
1866-1944

1. There is a place of qui - et rest, Near to the heart of God, A
2. There is a place of com - fort sweet, Near to the heart of God, A
3. There is a place of full re-lease, Near to the heart of God, A

place where sin can - not mo-lest, Near to the heart of God.
place where we our Sav - ior meet, Near to the heart of God.
place where all is joy and peace, Near to the heart of God.

Chorus

O Je - sus, blest Re - deem - er, Sent from the heart of God, Hold

us who wait be - fore Thee Near to the heart of God.

Pass Me Not

Fanny J. Crosby
1820-1915

William H. Doane
1832-1915

Hidden Peace

John S. Brown, 1899

L. O. Brown, 1899

1. I can-not tell thee whence it came, This peace with-in my breast; But
2. Be-neath the toil and care of life, This hid-den stream flows on; My
3. I can-not tell the half of love, Un-feigned, su-preme, di-vine. That

This I know, there fills my soul A strange and tran-quil rest.
wear-y soul no lon-ger thirsts, Nor am I sad and lone.
caused my dark-est in-most self With beams of hope to shine.

Chorus   Bright tempo

There's a deep set-tled peace in my soul, There's a deep set-tled peace in my soul; Tho' the

bil-lows of sin near me roll, He a-bides, Christ a-bides.

Wonderful Peace

W. D. Cornell 19th Cent.

W. G. Cooper
19th Cent.

o - ver my spir-it for-ev-er I pray, In fath- om-less bil-lows of love.

There's A River Of Life

L. Casebolt

There's a Riv-er of Life flow-ing out from me. Makes the lame to walk and the blind to see. O-pens pri-son doors, sets the cap - tives free. There's a Riv-er of Life flow-ing out from me!

Blessed Quietness

Marie P. Ferguson
19th century

W. S. Marshall
19th century

1. Joys are flow - ing like a riv - er, Since the Com - for-ter has come; He a-
2. Bring-ing life and health and glad - ness, All a - round this heav'n-ly Guest,
3. Like the rain that falls from heav - en, Like the sun - light from the sky, So the

bides with us for-ev - er, Makes the trust - ing heart His home.
un - be - lief and sad - ness, Changed our wea - ri - ness to rest.
Ho - ly Ghost is giv - en, Com - ing on us from on high.

Chorus

Bless - ed qui - et-ness, ho - ly qui - et-ness, What as-sur - ance in my soul! On the

storm - y sea, He speaks peace to me, How the bil - lows cease to roll!

Blessed Be The Name

Charles Wesley,
1707-1788

Ralph E. Hudson,
1843-1901

1. Bless - ed be the name,
2. Worth - y is the name,
3. Ho - ly is the name,
4. Je - sus is the name

Bless - ed be the name,

Bless - ed be the name of the Lord.

Bless - ed be the name,

Bless - ed be the name,

Bless - ed be the name of the Lord.

A - men.

Kum Ba Yah

Hark, 10,000 Harps

Thomas Kelly
1769-1854

Lowell Mason
1792-1872

1. Hark, ten thou - sand harps and voic - es Sound the note of praise a - bove; Je - sus reigns and heav'n re - joic - es, Je - sus reigns, the God of love; See, He sits on yon - der throne, Je - sus rules the word a - lone: Al - le - lu - ia! al - le - lu - ia! al - le - lu - ia! A - men.

2. Je - sus hail! whose glo - ry bright - ens All a - bove, and gives it worth; Lord of life, Thy smile en - light - ens, Cheers and charms Thy saints on earth; When we think of love like Thine, Lord, we own it love di - vine:

3. King of glo - ry, reign for - ev - er; Thine an ev - er - last - ing crown: Noth - ing from Thy love shall sev - er Those whom Thou hast made Thine own; Hap - py ob - jects of Thy grace, Des - tined to be - hold Thy face,

We Shall Praise The Name Of The Lord

Bill Bay

Here Comes Jesus

I Will Sing The Wondrous Story

Francis H. Rowley
1854-1952

Peter P. Bilhorn
1865-1936

1. I will sing the won-drous sto - ry Of the Christ who died for me How He
2. I was lost but Je-sus found me Found the sheep that went a-stray, Threw His
3. I was bruised but Je-sus healed me Faint was I from many a fall; Sight was

left His home in glo - ry For the cross of Cal - va - ry.
lov - ing arms a - round me, Drew me back in - to His way.
gone and fears pos-essed me, But He freed me from them all.

Chorus

Yes, I'll sing the won-drous sto - ry of the Christ who died for me, Sing it with the saints in glo - ry, Gath-ered

Come, Ye That Love The Lord

Isaac Watts
1674-1748

Aaron Williams
1731-1776

1. Come, we that love the Lord, And let our joys be known;
2. Let those re - fuse to sing Who nev - er knew our God;
3. The hill of Zi - on yields A thou - sand sa - cred sweets
4. Then let our songs a - bound And ev - 'ry tear be dry;

Join in a song with sweet ac - cords And thus sur - round the throne.
But chil - dren of the heav'n - ly King May speak their joys a - broad.
Be - fore we reach the heav'n - ly fields Or walk the gol - den streets.
We're march - ing thru Em - man - uel's ground To fair - er worlds on high. A - men.

Come Kingdom Of Our God

H. B. Johns

Wm A. Bay

Slowly

1. Come, king-dom of our God, Sweet reign of light and love! Shed
2. Sweep o'er our spir-its first Ex - tend thy heal-ing reign; There
3. Come, king-dom of our God! And make the broad earth Thine; Stretch
4. Soon may all tribes be blest With fruit from life's glad tree; And

peace and hope and joy a - broad, And wis - dom from a - bove.
raise and quench the sa - cred thirst, That nev - er pains a - gain.
o'er her lands and isles the rod That flowers with grace di - vine.
in its shade like bro - thers rest, Sons of one fam - i - ly.

He Is Lord

1. He is Lord,
2. He's my Lord, He is Lord, He is ris-en from the dead and He is Lord, Ev-'ry
3. You are Lord,

knee shall bow, Ev-'ry tongue con - fess that Je - sus Christ is Lord.

He Is My Everything

Composer Unknown

He is my ev - 'ry-thing He is my all.

He is my ev - 'ry-thing both great and small.

He gave His life for me made ev-'ry-thing new.

He is my ev - 'ry-thing now how a-bout you.

We're Marching To Zion

Isaac Watts 1674-1748
Chorus-Robert Lowry

Robert Lowry
1826-1899

I Stand On Zion's Mount

J. Swain From
"Spiritual Songs," 1881

William H. Walter
1825-1893

1. I stand on Zi - on's mount, And view my star - ry crown; No
2. The loft - y hills and towers, That lift their heads on high, Shall
3. The vault - ed heavens shall fall, Built by Je - ho - vah's hands; But

pow'r on earth can shake my hope, Nor hell can thrust me down!
all be lev - eled low in dust, Their ver - y names shall die.
fir - mer than the heav'ns, The Rock of my sal - va - tion stands! A - men.

The Hem Of His Garment

George F. Root
1820-1895

1. She on-ly touch'd the Hem of his gar-ment As to His side she stole, A-
2. She came in fear and trem-bling be-fore Him, She knew Her Lord had come; She
3. He turn'd with "Daugh-ter be of good com-fort, Thy faith hath made thee whole," And

mid the crowd that gath-ered a-round Him, And straight way she was whole.
felt that from Him vir-tue had healed her, The might-y deed was done.
peace that pass-eth all un-der-stand-ing With glad-ness filled her soul.

Chorus

Oh, touch the hem of His gar — ment And thou, too, shall be free; His

sav-ing pow'r this ver-y hour Shall give new life to thee.

106

I Know Whom I Have Believed

Daniel W. Whittle
1840-1901

James McGranahan
1840-1907

In The Garden

C. Austin Miles

1. I come to the gar-den a - lone, While the dew is still on the
2. He speaks, and the sound of His voice Is so sweet the birds hush their
3. I'd stay in the gar-den with Him Tho' the night a-round me be

ros - es, And the voice I hear fall-ing on my ear The Son of God dis-
sing - ing, And the mel - o-dy, that He gave to me With - in my heart is
fall - ing, But He bids me go; Thro' the voice of woe His voice to me is

Refrain

clos - es.
ring - ing.   And He walks with me and he talks with me, And He tells me I am His
call - ing.

own;   And the joy we share as we tar - ry there none oth - er has ev - er known.

© Copyright 1912 by Hall-Mack Co. © Renewed 1940. The Rodeheaver Co.
All Rights Reserved. International Copyright Secured. Used by Permission.

108

Chord

Major Key

Relative Minor

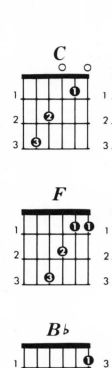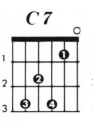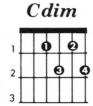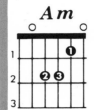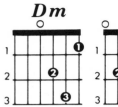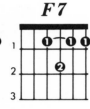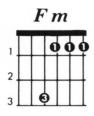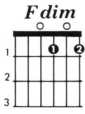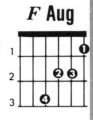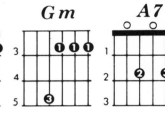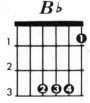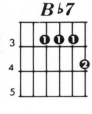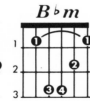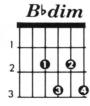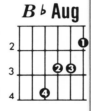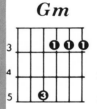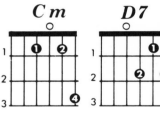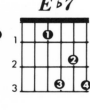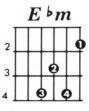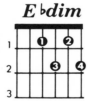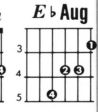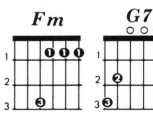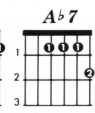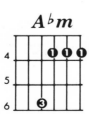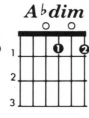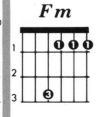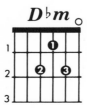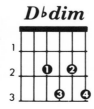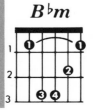

Chart

Major Key   Relative Minor

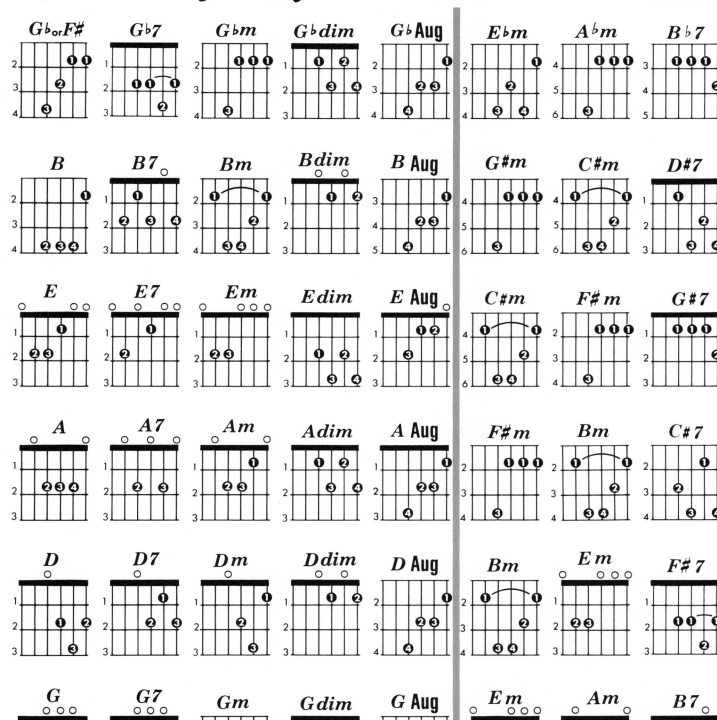